The

Yes You Can

Man

by

Williams Oshen

For Avery Oshen and Triton William, who offer a daily reminder that a mind full of hopes leaves no room for nopes.

ISBN-13: 978-1481192866

ISBN-10: 1481192868

Printed in the U.S.A.

On the first day of never, I created a plan.

A jaw-dropping, eye-popping, masterful plan.

A wildly confusing and mildly amusing with no room for losing,

Yes You Can Plan.

On the next day of never they said, "It won't work!

Give up what you're doing. Your brain's gone berserk!

It's crazy. Too hazy. Too wacky. Too dumb.

Too tough to envision what it might become."

When they said, "No way!" I said, "Just watch me go.

I'm the Yes You Can Man and I've no time for NO!"

On the next day of never I built a small shop.

I made a bright sign, and I put it on top.

Then I looked at my plan...my Yes You Can Plan...

and I lit up my sign that said Yes You Can Man!

Then I emptied my store, made it bare as could be,

with only a sofa for one, two, or three.

In no time at all people lined down the street,

to see this new shop with just one love seat.

People would come just to hear the word YES,

so crippled by nay-sayers stressing their stress.

The first one in line was young Molly Mamoose,

who wanted to make and sell Kurdish Kazoos.

Her friends said, "It's silly. There's no one to buy.

Don't waste your money. Don't even try."

She came and she asked me, "Can I succeed?

Can I sell Kurdish Kazoos at top speed?"

I told her she could and I told her she would

if she stuck to her plan and she made her plan good...

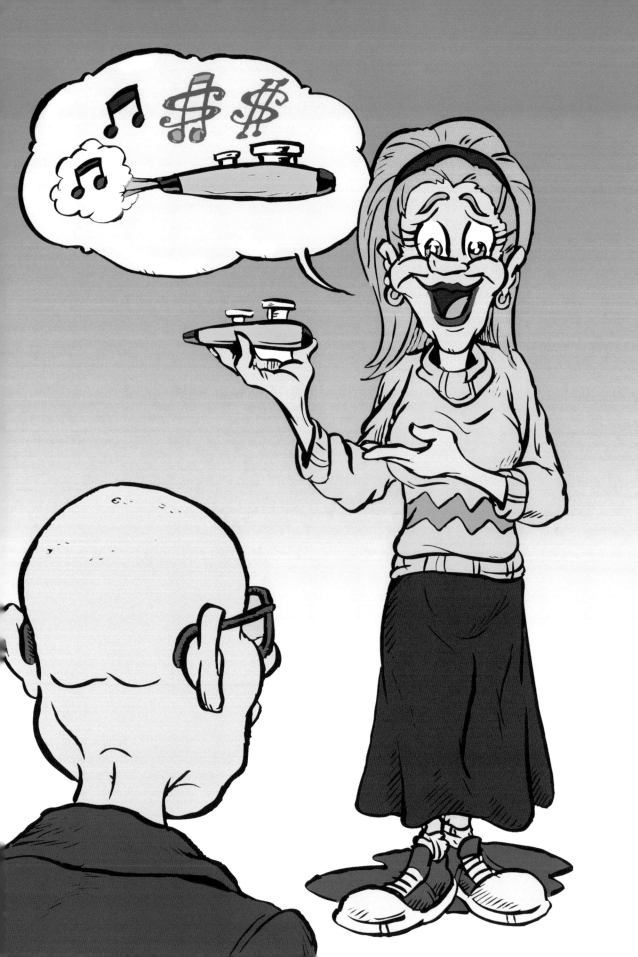

"It might not be easy. It might not be quick.

It might make you tired, or crabby or sick.

It might take some tweaking or twisting or turning.

It might take some changing and mind bending learning.

You might need to move when others say, "Stop!"

You might need to flip, when others say, "Flop."

You might need to sweat and you might need to bleed

If you want to sell Kurdish Kazoos at top speed."

The next one to come was old Finnegan Flynn,

who wanted to retire in North Michigan.

He thought it too late for his dream to come true

since his friends all told him it's too hard to do.

He came and he asked me, "Can it be done?

Can I, at my age, retire and have fun?"

I told him he could and I told him he would

if he stuck to his plan and he made his plan good...

"The world is chock-full of some people doing

what others waste all of their free time pooh-poohing.

So be busy working while they're busy stressing...

while they're busy NO-ing, be busy YES-ing.

You'll need finely tuned focus on a finely tuned plan

if you hope to retire in North Michigan."

The next one to come on the next day of never

was Harriett Hinkleman, who'd invented a lever.

Her friends had assured her she'd never sell levers

but she wasn't sure that she'd never sell levers.

She came and she asked me, "Can I sell levers?"

As I wasn't sure if she could sell levers

I asked her to ask herself, "Can I sell levers?"

If she answered, "Never," she'd never sell levers.

As long as she thought that she'd never sell levers

she'd never sell levers forevers and evers.

When she replied, "Yes, I can sell levers,"

I replied, "Yes, you can sell levers."

The next day of never was more of the same.

People came and they came and they came and they came.

They came for the reasons that all people would.

They came for reminders that yes they sure could.

I told them to not confuse CAN NOT with DON'T,

or DID NOT or WILL NOT or WOULD NOT or WON'T.

I told them to not give up thinking they COULDN'T

if really they DIDN'T 'cause simply they WOULDN'T.

And then an idea crept into my head

to do something different the next day instead.

I shuttered the windows, locked all the doors,

drew all the blinds, and covered the floors...

I threw out my sofa and rewired my sign

to only light up when someone pressed shine,

and put in a nickel...a nickel times nine.

A nickel times nine from each one in line

on that next day of never...

and never times nine.

And people still came, even more than before,

to drop their nine nickels through the slot on the door.

I glanced at the plan that had led to this feat

as I sauntered away from the crowds on the street.

I wondered what all those would think of me now,

who looked at my plan and said, "There's no how."

Maybe they thought it just wasn't specific...

with only three words it just couldn't be terrific.

Or maybe they thought it just wasn't a plan

with no other words except oh *Yes You Can*...

Whatever the reason, I really can't say.

But doubters are sure to put NO in the way.

And NO has no place in a Yes You Can Plan,

and no space in the life of a Yes You Can Man.

Made in the USA
Lexington, KY
07 February 2013